APATOSAURUS

REVISED EDITION

A **TRUE BOOK**

by

Elaine Landau

Children's Press®

A Division of Scholastic Inc.

New York Toronto London Auckland Sydney
Mexico City New Delhi Hong Kong
Danbury, Connecticut

Apatosaurus was a huge dinosaur.

Content Consultant
Susan H. Gray, MS, Zoology,
Little Rock, Arkansas

Reading Consultant
Cecilia Minden-Cupp, PhD
Former Director, Language and Literacy Program Harvard Graduate School of Education

Author's Dedication
For Julia

The photograph on the cover and the title page shows an Apatosaurus model in the Dinosaur Prehistoric Park in Calgary, Alberta, Canada.

Library of Congress Cataloging-in-Publication Data
Landau, Elaine.
    Apatosaurus / by Elaine Landau. — Rev. ed.
        p. cm. — (A true book)
    Includes bibliographical references and index.
    ISBN-10: 0-531-16799-2 (lib. bdg.)   0-531-15469-6 (pbk.)
    ISBN-13: 978-0-531-16799-1 (lib. bdg.)   978-0-531-15469-4 (pbk.)
    1. Apatosaurus—Juvenile literature. I. Title. II. Series.
QE862.S3L36 2007
567.913'8–dc22

2006004423

CHILDREN'S PRESS, and A TRUE BOOK™, and associated logos are trademarks and/or registered trademarks of Scholastic Library Publishing. SCHOLASTIC and associated logos are trademarks and/or registered trademarks of Scholastic Inc.
1 2 3 4 5 6 7 8 9 10 R 16 15 14 13 12 11 10 09 08 07

Contents

Earth looked much different 150 million years ago than it does today.

Picture This

You have traveled back 150 million years in time. It is the Age of the Dinosaurs. There are no people. Huge leathery-skinned **reptiles** wander Earth.

In the distance, you see an **enormous** dinosaur coming

your way. You are looking at one of the largest creatures that ever lived. It weighs 33 tons, or about as much as eighty-five hippos.

This dinosaur is really long, too. It measures nearly 80 feet (24 meters) from head to tail. That is longer than two school buses placed end to end.

The ground begins to shake. The dinosaur is getting closer. You hear the loud

For a long time, scientists
believed *Apatosaurus* ate
leaves from the tops of
tall trees. We now know
that *Apatosaurus* could
not reach that high.

noise this creature makes as it moves along. This dinosaur used to be called *Brontosaurus*, which means "thunder lizard." Today, it is called *Apatosaurus*. In this book, you will learn many interesting facts about *Apatosaurus*. If you would like to know more about *Apatosaurus*—read on.

Hey, Big Guy

Apatosaurus looked like what most people think of when they hear the word *dinosaur*. Four sturdy legs supported this dinosaur's huge body. Its front legs were shorter than its hind, or back, legs. This caused its body to slope downward from its hips to its neck.

   Apatosaurus's body was a little like a suspension bridge. On a suspension bridge, the roadway hangs from wire cables attached to high towers.

On *Apatosaurus*, the stomach, heart, lungs, and chest muscles hung from its shoulders. The shoulders were like the towers of the suspension bridge. They held up the biggest part of the animal.

The heaviest part of *Apatosaurus* was its middle, between its front legs and tail.

This view of an elephant's foot shows what *Apatosaurus*'s feet looked like.

Apatosaurus's short, broad feet have sometimes been compared to an elephant's. Like an elephant, *Apatosaurus* had five **stubby** toes on each

12

foot. But this dinosaur also had a large claw on its big toes.

Apatosaurus had a very long neck and tail, too. So you might think this dinosaur had a huge head. Well, guess what? *Apatosaurus* had a small head for an animal its size. Its head was shaped like a football and was about the size of two footballs placed next to each other. *Apatosaurus*'s brain was only about the size of an apple.

Apatosaurus had eyes toward the back of its head and nostrils at the top.

Like all dinosaurs, *Apatosaurus* was a **prehistoric** reptile. Yet its face did not look much like the faces of reptiles you see today. *Apatosaurus*'s eyes were set far back in its head, and its nostrils were near the top of its head.

Super Tail!

Perhaps the most amazing part of *Apatosaurus*'s body was its tail. An *Apatosaurus* tail made up nearly one-third of its length. The tail was about 30 feet (9 m) long. This is about as long as five men lying head to toe. With eighty-two bones linked

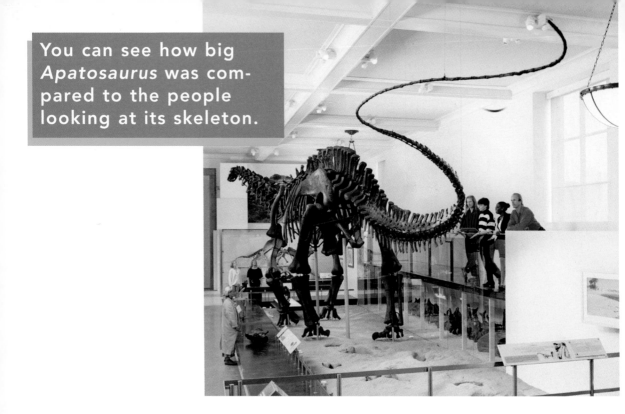

You can see how big *Apatosaurus* was compared to the people looking at its skeleton.

together, the tail was also quite heavy. However, *Apatosaurus*'s large tail may have balanced the dinosaur's very long neck.

An *Apatosaurus* tail was broad at the base and narrow at the tip. It looked like a giant

Two Names, One Dinosaur

For a long time, *Apatosaurus* was known as *Brontosaurus*. Othniel Charles Marsh, a scientist who studied prehistoric life, described and named *Apatosaurus* in 1877. Then in 1879, he described and named another dinosaur, *Brontosaurus*. However, it was later discovered that *Brontosaurus* and *Apatosaurus* were the same dinosaur. Since the dinosaur had been named *Apatosaurus* first, that's what it is called today.

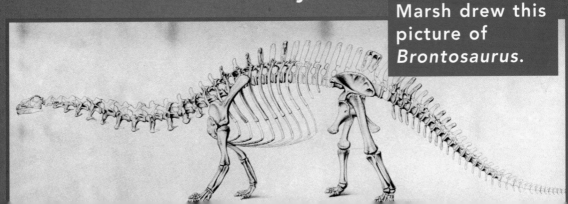

Marsh drew this picture of *Brontosaurus*.

whip. *Apatosaurus*'s tail could swing like a whip, too. By stomping its feet, the animal could toss its tail from side to side. *Apatosaurus*'s strong back muscles gave the tail a very powerful swing.

The Life of Apatosaurus

Apatosaurus lived in western North America. Its **fossils** have been uncovered in Colorado, Utah, Oklahoma, and Wyoming. Fossils are evidence of plants and animals that lived long ago. Fossils might include bones, footprints, teeth, or leaf

MONTANA

IDAHO

WYOMING

NEBRASKA

UTAH

COLORADO

KANSAS

ARIZONA

NEW MEXICO

OKLAHOMA

TEXAS

MEXICO

UNITED STATES

The lightest area on this map shows areas where *Apatosaurus* fossils have been found.

A herd of traveling *Apatosaurus*

imprints on rocks. Scientists
use fossils to learn about
dinosaurs like *Apatosaurus*.

Paleontologists—scientists
who study prehistoric life—
believe that *Apatosaurus*
lived and traveled in herds,

21

or groups. There may have been as many as twenty dinosaurs in a herd. Together, they roamed the land searching for new feeding grounds.

It was important to *Apatosaurus*'s survival to be part of a herd because the animals could protect each other. *Apatosaurus* was large, but it could not outrun its enemies. Enemies were less likely to attack a herd than an animal that was alone.

Fossil footprints from a herd of *Apatosaurus*

Paleontologists think that *Apatosaurus* herds may have acted as elephant herds do when threatened. The adults in the herd probably tried to protect their young. It is possible that the male dinosaurs formed a circle, shielding the young dinosaurs and females within. *Apatosaurus* was not completely defenseless. The claws on its front feet could be useful against an enemy. *Apatosaurus* may also have

Apatosaurus could defend itself against attacks by other dinosaurs.

been able to badly injure another dinosaur with a swing of its huge tail.

The Wonders

Today, paleontologists know more about dinosaurs than ever before. They can now make computer models of these prehistoric creatures. Computer models can provide valuable information about how the animals moved about.

Working on a computer is easier than handling fossils. Often fossil bones are huge. A single dinosaur bone can weigh 100 pounds

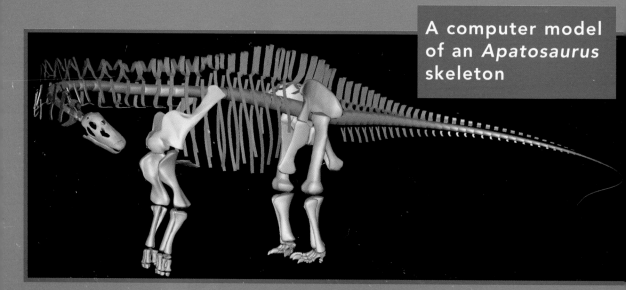

A computer model of an *Apatosaurus* skeleton

# of Computers

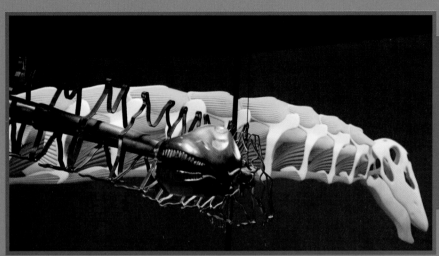

This model of *Apatosaurus* (foreground) is based on the computer model in the background.

(45 kilograms). Even when fossils are put together, it is still hard for paleontologists to understand exactly how dinosaurs moved.

Computer models of these bones tell us much more. For example, paleontologists now know that *Apatosaurus* could easily bend and turn its neck. It could even look backward!

Apatosaurus stands on its hind legs to fight off *Allosaurus*.

In some cases, *Apatosaurus* might have even reared up on its hind legs to thrash an attacker. However, paleontologists doubt that it did this often. It would have been hard for *Apatosaurus* to keep its balance. Its enemy would have surely won the struggle if *Apatosaurus* toppled over during the fight.

Feeding Time!

Apatosaurus was an herbivore, or plant eater. It was among the largest herbivores in the world at the time. Unlike flesh-eating dinosaurs, *Apatosaurus* was unable to take huge mouthfuls of food. Its jaws were too small. So to feed its giant body, *Apatosaurus* probably had to eat throughout the day. There must have been little time for other activities.

This *Apatosaurus* skull shows how small the animal's jaws were.

Paleontologists once thought that *Apatosaurus* simply lifted its head to pull leaves from the tallest tree-tops. However, they now believe that this dinosaur could not have reached that high. It is far more likely that it grazed on low-growing plants and ferns.

These dinosaurs also may have eaten plants growing in shallow water. It is likely that they stood on the edge of

Apatosaurus probably ate only the plants that grew close to the ground.

Apatosaurus feeding on swamp plants

swamps and lakes and reached down into the water with their long necks. Having shorter front legs would allow them to stand comfortably that way.

What a Dinosaur

In 1909, dinosaur researcher Earl Douglas was digging for fossils on a sandstone ledge on the Green River in Utah. There he uncovered a nearly complete skeleton of *Apatosaurus*. It was a thrilling find! Paleontologists finally could see what *Apatosaurus* looked like.

This sandstone area in the Utah portion of Dinosaur National Monument is rich in dinosaur fossils.

Although *Apatosaurus* had teeth, it did not chew its food. Instead, it swallowed its meals whole. First, however, the dinosaur swallowed some rocks and pebbles. These pebbles are sometimes called stomach stones. They tore up the tough plant matter when it reached the animal's stomach. Once the food was mashed into a thick paste, it was ready to be digested.

Our Changing World

Today, there are no living dinosaurs left. Only fossils of skeletons or models of these huge creatures remain. Some people mistakenly think that all dinosaurs became **extinct**, or died out, at the same time. That is not the way it happened.

It took about a million years
for all the dinosaurs to die out.
For about 180 million years,
various kinds of dinosaurs
existed. Yet no single kind of
dinosaur lasted the entire time
that dinosaurs were on Earth.

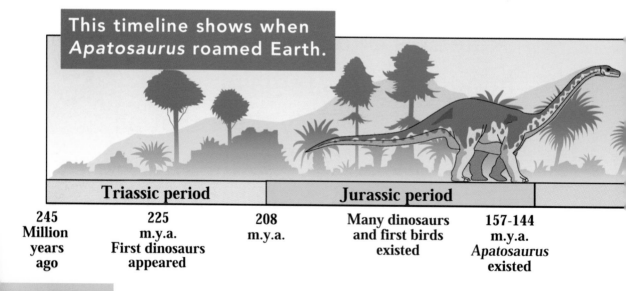

This timeline shows when *Apatosaurus* roamed Earth.

	Triassic period		Jurassic period	
245 Million years ago	225 m.y.a. First dinosaurs appeared	208 m.y.a.	Many dinosaurs and first birds existed	157-144 m.y.a. *Apatosaurus* existed

There is no definite answer to why the dinosaurs became extinct. During the Age of the Dinosaurs, Earth was still changing. The large landmasses called continents had not finished forming.

(Note:"m.y.a." means "million years ago")

| Cretaceous period | Tertiary period | |

65
m.y.a.
Last dinosaurs
became extinct

1.6
m.y.a.
First humans
appeared

Seas and mountain ranges were still taking shape. Different kinds of plant life appeared. It is likely that dinosaurs couldn't get used to all these changes.

Many paleontologists think the dinosaurs became extinct after an asteroid crashed into Earth. Asteroids are large, rocky, planetlike bodies that move through space. If an asteroid struck Earth, a huge crater, or hole, would have been created.

Museum models help us imagine what real *Apatosaurus* were like.

The dust from the hole would have floated up into the **atmosphere** to form thick, dark clouds. These clouds would have blocked out the sun. Earth would have become very cold. The dinosaurs probably could not have survived the cold temperatures.

Apatosaurus lasted on Earth for more than 10 million years. Paleontologists past and present have studied its

A paleontologist at the University of Wyoming studies part of an *Apatosaurus* skeleton.

fossils. This giant dinosaur is part of the story of our changing world.

To Find Out More

Here are some additional resources to help you learn more about *Apatosaurus*:

 **Books**

Benton, Michael. **Giant Plant Eaters**. Copper Beech Books, 2001.

Gray, Susan H. **Apatosaurus**. Child's World, 2004.

Harris, Nicholas. **The Incredible Journey Through the World of the Dinosaurs**. Peter Bendrick Books, 2002.

Jay, Michael. **Age of the Dinosaurs**. Raintree, 2004.

Scott, Janine. **Discovering Dinosaurs**. Compass Point Books, 2002.

Organizations and Online Sites

Dinosaur National Monument
4545 E. Highway 40
Dinosaur, CO 81610-9724
http://www.nps.gov/dino

There's a lot to do at this site, including a virtual tour of the park's museum. You can also watch a slide show to follow a fossil from discovery to study and display.

Enchanted Learning— Apatosaurus
http://www.enchantedlearning.com/subjects/dinosaurs/dinos/Apatosaurus.html

Learn more about how this long-necked dinosaur looked and lived.

Project Exploration
950 East 61st Street
Chicago, IL 60637
http://www.info@project exploration.org

This organization works to increase students' interest in paleontology.

Scholastic—Dinosaurs!
http://www.teacher.scholastic.com/activities/dinosaurs

Check out this fun Web site for dinosaur lovers! Take a dinosaur tour, build a dinosaur, and don't miss the dinosaur quiz.

Important Words

atmosphere the blanket of gases that surrounds Earth

enormous very large

extinct no longer existing

fossils evidence of plants and animals that lived long ago. Fossils might include bones, footprints, teeth, or leaf imprints on rocks.

prehistoric from the time before history was recorded

reptiles cold-blooded animals that crawl on the ground or creep on short legs

stubby short and thick

Index

Meet the Author

Award-winning author Elaine Landau worked as a newspaper reporter, an editor, and a youth-services librarian before becoming a full-time writer. She has written more than 250 nonfiction books for young people, including True Books on animals, countries, and food. Ms. Landau has a bachelor's degree in English and journalism from New York University as well as a master's degree in library and information science. She lives with her husband and son in Miami, Florida.

Photographs © 2007: Alamy Images/Wally Bauman: cover, 1; American Museum of Natural History: 34 (#2417); AP/Wide World Photos/Mary Altaffer: 27; Carnegie Museum of Natural History: 31; IPN Stock Images/Louie Psihoyos: 16, 17; DinoMorph™ by Kent A. Stevens, University of Oregon: 26; Museum of the Rockies/Bruce Selyem: 41; Natural History Museum, London: 2 (Neave Parker), 7 (John Sibbick); Photo Researchers, NY: 23, 35, 43 (Francois Gohier), 10, 11 (Laurie O'Keefe); PictureQuest/Highlights for Children: 21; The Image Works/Mary Evans Picture Library: 4, 25; Visuals Unlimited: 33 (Ken Lucas), 12 (Milton H. Tierney Jr.).

Map by Bob Italiano
Timeline and illustrations by Greg Harris